Programme and Project Management Library

An Introduction to Programme Management

London: HMSO

The Government Centre for Information Systems

An Introduction to Programme Management

© Crown Copyright 1993

Application for reproduction should be made to HMSO

First published 1993

ISBN 0 11 330611 3

For further information regarding this publication
and other CCTA products please contact:

Library
CCTA
Riverwalk House
157-161 Millbank
London SW1P 4RT

071-217 3331

Contents

Foreword

1 About this volume   1

    1.1 Purpose of this volume

    1.2 Who should read this volume

    1.3 Structure of the volume

2 Overview of programme management   3

    2.1 What is programme management?

    2.2 Why is programme management needed?

    2.3 What is the approach proposed?

    2.4 How does programme management differ from project management?

    2.5 Programme management and strategy implementation

    2.6 Benefits of programme management

3 Key principles   9

    3.1 Principles of the approach

    3.2 When to use the approach

    3.3 Selecting and planning a programme

    3.4 Principles for managing a programme

    3.5 Senior management leadership

    3.6 Key supporting roles

    3.7 A framework to support change management

4	**Programme management activities**	**19**
	4.1 Four phases of activities	
	4.2 Phase 1 - Programme Identification	
	4.3 Phase 2 - Programme Definition	
	4.4 Phase 3 - Programme Execution	
	4.5 Phase 4 - Benefits Realisation	
5	**Organising the programme**	**25**
	5.1 Programme Director role	
	5.2 Programme Executive roles	
	5.3 Business Change Manager responsibilities	
	5.4 Programme Manager responsibilities	
	5.5 Design Authority responsibilities	
	5.6 Programme Support Office	
	5.7 Roles at the boundaries of programme management	
6	**Lessons from practical application**	**31**
	6.1 Identifying change points	
	6.2 Keeping the business operation running	
	6.3 Scoping fundamental programmes	
	6.4 Accommodating change	
Bibliography		**33**

Foreword

This volume is a part of CCTA's **Programme and Project Management Library**.

The common theme for the library's contents is the subject of Programme and Project Management. The library covers a wide range of issues relating to the effective management of programmes and projects so as to meet the needs of the organisation. Expressed simply, at the programme level this means effectively co-ordinating a portfolio of projects to deliver the full range of anticipated benefits for the business; at the project level this means the delivery of quality products on time and within budget.

Collectively, the volumes in this library cover the needs of a broad audience, ranging from senior decision-makers who seek high-level "what" and "why" guidance, through to active practitioners of detailed techniques and approaches who seek "how-to" guidance. The volumes complement the guidance contained within PRINCE, CCTA's project management method which is published separately.

The Programme and Project Management Library is one of a series of themed libraries produced by CCTA which address the needs of business managers and information systems professionals. If you require further information, or have views on this or other publications within the library, please contact:

Customer Services
Information Systems Engineering Group
CCTA
Gildengate House
Upper Green Lane
NORWICH
NR3 1DW

An Introduction to Programme Management

Chapter 1
About this volume

1 About this volume

1.1 Purpose of this volume

Management of large-scale change can bring particular problems in co-ordinating a complex and wide ranging set of projects and achieving the planned benefits. The purpose of this volume is to explain how programme management provides an approach for organisations that are facing the need to introduce large-scale changes.

The volume outlines the general concepts of programme management and describes how the organisation, structures, activities and products of the approach will help managers to implement complex business change successfully.

1.2 Who should read the volume

Its intended readers are managers who are responsible for implementing large-scale business change or for managing multiple projects and the complexities which can arise. This may include:

- members of the Management Board who will be responsible for selecting programmes and appointing Programme Directors

- Project Board members, if they are to implement their projects within a programme

- those responsible for planning and operating support services – for example, accommodation or IT services, or for setting technical policies and standards

- line managers whose business is affected by a change programme and who may be involved in implementing that programme.

This guidance will also be of interest to the management services and IS/IT services industry.

1.3 Structure of the volume

Following this introductory chapter, an Overview chapter provides a definition of Programme Management, explains when and where it is relevant and describes the benefits it can bring.

Three further chapters then set out how the approach can help business change succeed:

- the first explains the key principles on which this guidance is based
- the second very briefly outlines the activities involved in conducting a programme
- the third describes the roles and responsibilities required for organising a programme.

This *Introduction to Programme Management* is complemented by a complete handbook describing how to set up and run programmes called *A Guide to Programme Management*. Both are volumes from CCTA's Programme and Project Management Library, available from HMSO. Programme Management issues are highlighted in a CCTA briefing pamphlet for senior management: *Managing Programmes of Large-Scale Change*.

2 Overview of programme management

2.1 What is programme management?

Programme management is the co-ordinated management of a portfolio of projects to achieve a set of business objectives. Programme management provides a framework for implementing business strategies and initiatives and for managing multiple projects.

2.2 Why is programme management needed?

Public sector bodies have to respond to many kinds of change, such as:

- government-wide initiatives such as the Citizen's Charter and change arising out of UK and European legislation

- departmental initiatives, such as efficiency scrutinies and relocation, and the introduction of new types of business process

- increasing use of contracting out, market testing, and more generally the creation of *arm's length* relationships between *service demanders* and *service suppliers* within government.

Such changes affect work patterns, culture, the roles and responsibilities of individuals, the way in which they are organised, their needs for information systems, and perhaps above all, the way in which public bodies serve their customers.

The sheer variety and number of projects underway in response to change can cause real problems of:

- objectives and benefits that are impossible to tie directly to the individual projects being implemented and are anyway beyond the real authority or responsibility of the project's manager to deliver

- excessive costs and time over-runs, caused by insufficient co-ordination of projects, where those concerned may often be aware that dependencies exist but do not have effective mechanisms for managing them

- plans that are driven by the work schedules of those designing and implementing the changes, not by the effective assimilation of change into the workplace for maximum benefits from the investment

- an overload of changes for those in the business environment, whose first priority is to keep the ongoing business operation running efficiently, economically, and effectively, irrespective of change.

2.3 What is the approach proposed?

In this volume, programme management is defined as follows:

> PROGRAMME MANAGEMENT is the selection and planning of a portfolio of projects to achieve a set of business objectives; and the efficient execution of these projects within a controlled environment such that they realise maximum benefit for the resulting business operation.

Projects are the means by which resources can be deployed to produce 'products' (tangible deliverables such as buildings or computer systems) and also 'softer' results such as new competences in staff. The portfolio of projects within a programme may cover both tangible products and softer results. Each project should be carefully scoped and should be of a manageable size. Programmes will not succeed unless they are underpinned by a controlled environment of strong project management disciplines.

Programmes should be selected and planned to improve the operation of one or more business areas. A single business area may, in a small department or agency, cover all its activities. In a larger organisation, it is more likely that there will be a number of separate business areas, for example those which serve different types of customer, or which are implementing different legislation, or those performed by front and back offices.

The benefits of a programme arise from the enhanced efficiency, economy and effectiveness of the business operation compared with the current operation.

Chapter 2
Overview of programme management

2.4 How does programme management differ from project management?

Projects deliver products. Such products *enable* improvements in business operations; they are not objectives in their own right. Programme managers should take a broader and more flexible view than project managers; they should be concerned to achieve not only product delivery, but also the actual realisation of benefits. The benefits from individual projects may not arise until after project completion (and will therefore lie beyond the scope of the project's control). Programmes therefore need to continue until the transition from current to new business operation is complete.

Programme management disciplines provide an umbrella under which a number of projects can be managed but they supplement, rather than replace, project management. Some key differences between project management and programme management are:

> Project management:
>
> - is an intense and focused activity that is 'driven' by the products that are to be delivered
>
> - includes change control mechanisms but is best suited to objectives that are closely bounded and relatively certain
>
> - is suited to deliver a product.
>
> Programme management:
>
> - is a broadly spread activity that uses a process approach and is concerned with more broadly defined objectives
>
> - is suited to orchestrating large numbers of component projects and activities with complex and changing inter-relationships, in an uncertain environment (that is, a larger and more dynamic environment)
>
> - is suited to managing the impact of and the benefits from a number of component products and ensuring that there is a smooth transition into a new business operation.

An Introduction to Programme Management

2.5 Programme management and strategy implementation

Figure 1 below illustrates the relationship between strategies, programmes and projects.

All organisations should have an enduring and corporate statement of purpose (a Mission Statement), and Aims and Objectives that state the long term goals in support of the mission. Strategies and initiatives refine the aims and objectives in the light of specific business requirements and describe how the aims and objectives are to be achieved. Strategies and initiatives are generally defined too broadly to be taken forward directly as projects.

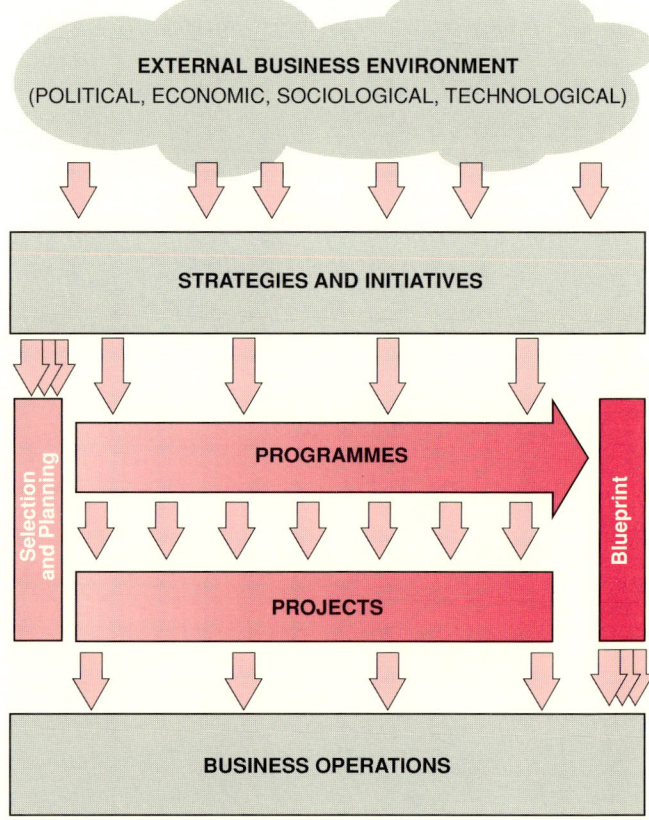

Figure 1 The programme management environment

Chapter 2
Overview of programme management

Programme management activities and documentation fill the gap:

- between the broad focus of the strategy level and the greater detail which is necessary to begin a project or projects

- between the terminology used by business areas and that used by functional specialists such as systems engineers, accountants, or estates managers

- between the user-side emphasis on the final business processes, objectives and benefits required by business area managers and the supplier-side emphasis on the infrastructure and support services (which incidentally may have their own technical policies and plans)

- between concern for the broad strategic change associated with transition to a new business operation and the necessary narrow focus on managing the specific activity and resource targets of projects.

2.6 Benefits of programme management

The main advantages from adopting a programme management approach to large-scale change initiatives include the following:

- more effective delivery of changes because they are planned and implemented in an integrated way for the business users

- effective response to disparate initiatives from the top down, filling the gap between business and IS strategies, and between strategies and projects

- support for senior management to keep activities focused on *business change objectives*

- improved resource management and project integration

An Introduction to Programme Management

- better management of risk and project prioritisation, because the wider context is understood and explicitly acknowledged

- help to achieve real business benefits through a formal process of their management and measurement

- improved control through a framework within which the costs of introducing new infrastructure, standards, and quality regimes can be justified, measured and assessed.

3 Key principles

3.1 Principles of the approach

Programmes should be selected and planned to target the operation of a whole business area (or of more than one) and must be led by senior managers, whose commitment and involvement are essential. By adopting programme management, those senior managers will find it easier to:

- clarify how their new business operation will deliver
- build and maintain a business case which clearly compares current business operations with more beneficial future business operations
- define and drive through the transition from current to future operation
- identify, assess and manage risks
- introduce and enforce a consistent system of quality management, policies and standards.

3.2 When to use the approach

Programme Management should be used when one or more of the following conditions apply.

Shared objectives

- there is a need to co-ordinate several initiatives affecting a business area
- the proposed projects support a strategy, a strategic change or a similar type of initiative, with significant impact on the organisation
- a set of proposed projects and activities address a common problem or deliver a common set of business benefits

Management of complex change

- the set of changes cannot be managed as a single project because of size or complexity

- the set of changes covers too wide a range of business areas or development skills for a conventional project management structure

- there are strong interdependencies between projects that require co-ordinated management

Shared resources

- the use of resources from a common pool can be optimised by co-ordination across projects

Advantages of scale

- the grouping of projects gives cost savings by avoiding duplication of effort

- the grouping of projects provides the increase in scale to justify necessary infrastructure

- the grouping of projects justifies the employment, recruitment or training of specialist skill groups

- the grouping of projects leads to risk reduction – for example, by closely controlling vulnerable project interfaces.

3.3 Selecting and planning a programme

Figure 2 opposite illustrates the way in which programme management is applied to deliver benefits from changes to business operations. At the top of the model strategies or initiatives provide aims, objectives and policies to guide the developments below. At the bottom, the operational line businesses and the supporting functions deliver their services. In between, a change programme comprising a portfolio of projects helps to move the business forward from the current business operation to the future, improved, business operation by creating new products, which can include facilities, services, or changed staff behaviours (for example through training). These products move into the business operation as they are completed.

Chapter 3
Key principles

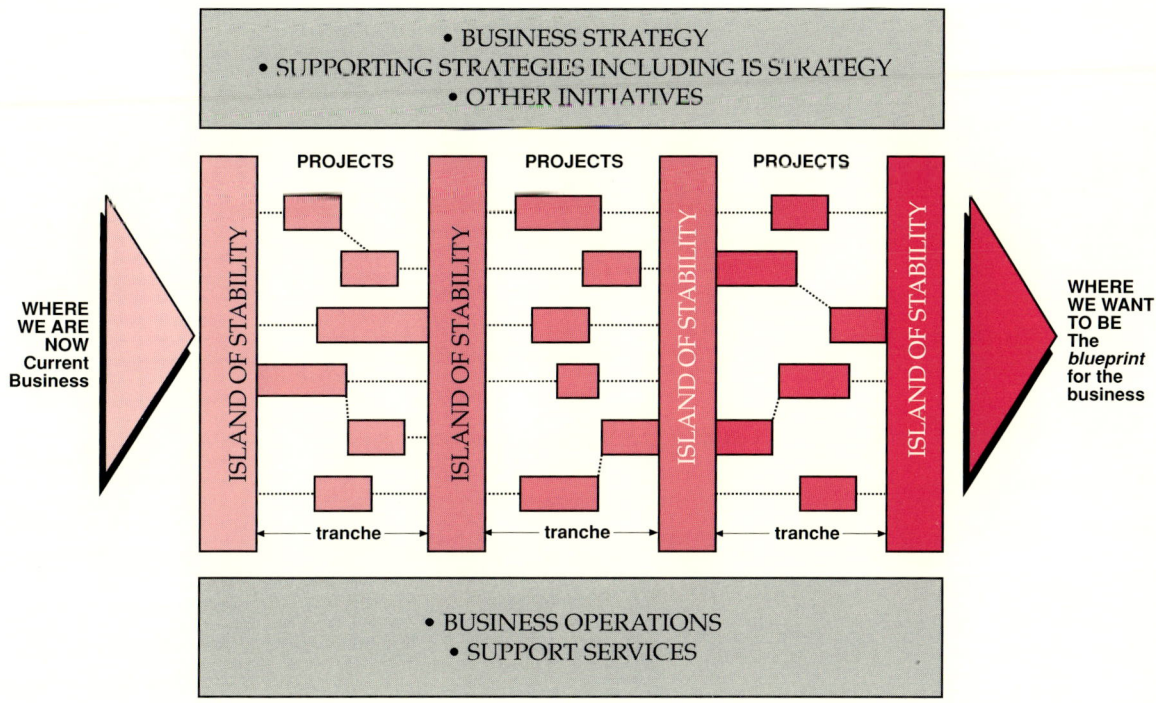

Figure 2 A model of programme management

A critical initial decision must be to *define the boundaries* of the programme and its target business operation. The model illustrates how the principles for selecting and planning a programme, described below, may be applied most beneficially.

At the top of the model   Typically the strategies for business, information systems, support services, staffing, and other resources will all have generated separate implementation plans and usually also separate business cases. At the same time, most organisations have several current initiatives which although not articulated as strategies have a similar impact on the business. For example there may be an initiative to reduce costs, improve performance, or respond to a piece of government legislation. Benefits proposed for the respective strategies and initiatives will be described only in broad outline; but several initiatives may often seek improvements in the same operational areas (for example through cost savings).

A key function of a programme is to integrate these implementation plans and initiatives into a co-ordinated change plan for the business operation.

By defining a programme of work that may draw down projects from more than one strategy, but related to the same business area, it is possible to identify benefits in terms to which line managers and their staff can readily relate, and to which commitment can be more readily generated.

A key responsibility of a programme management team will be to formulate a clear model of the improved business operation (this can be thought of as a *blueprint* for the business) which must be maintained and managed throughout the course of programme implementation.

The programme management team must plan the business transition path for the operational areas from current operations to the future operations.

The middle layer

Transition from current to future operations will normally be achieved best via tranches of work; for example, to take early benefits, to increase the skills of the workforce by manageable degrees, or simply because of uncertainty as to the best means by which to proceed until feasibility has been established and options identified and appraised.

At the end of each tranche, the programme's management team should review progress, assess benefits, risks and remaining uncertainty and further refine the objectives and requirements in the light of this information. At this review point ('Island of Stability') plans for the next tranche can then be made. Where a need for a significant change of direction is identified, this may have an impact at the strategic level and on the *blueprint*.

Chapter 3
Key principles

Between the projects there will be interfaces and inter-dependencies. Where projects' objectives evolve and scopes change during execution, action will be needed to re-align projects and allocate resources between them.

A number of the projects in the change programme may comprise developments that need to be co-ordinated by the programme's procedures to ensure the technical integrity and consistency of the whole programme.

At the bottom of the model Projects may deliver the means to achieve benefits, but benefits will actually be realised by operational use of the project deliverables. Successful integration of project deliverables into the business operation will need very positive management action in order to realise these benefits.

Each project will typically enable only a proportion of the total benefits planned for the overall programme to be realised; some (for example infrastructure projects or the introduction of standards) may not contribute benefits directly, as individual projects, at all. When the projects are managed as a programme, it is easier to co-ordinate their outputs to deliver all the benefits obtainable for the business operation.

As projects are completed and made operational, they may introduce changes into the underlying operational support services; for example new IS applications may require increased IT network capacity. The programme management team plans and monitors the implementation of such changes and ensures that all projects conform to the organisation's policies and standards and that operational service levels are maintained and improved. This programme management activity helps to ensure that all new business processes that are created are fully supportable in the operational environment.

3.4 Principles for managing a programme

Experience of implementing large-scale change programmes in a wide range of public and private sector organisations shows that successful management has been based on a set of common principles:

- the programme must be led by a *programme director* at a sufficiently senior level to make things happen

- the *programme director* must be effectively supported so that there is active management of:
    - the change in business operations
    - the business benefits targeted by the programme
    - the efficient co-ordination of the projects within the programme
    - the integration with design of systems and architectures that span the whole organisation (for example, a technical IT architecture, a new pay and grading regime)
    - the handover of completed projects to the business operational services

- the approach must provide a framework that allows the programme to be managed flexibly and responsively, and enables well-informed, top-down decision making, regarding change, quality and risks.

3.5 Senior management leadership

An essential part of the philosophy of the approach to programme management is that line management should take full responsibility for programmes of expenditure in their business areas, even for such technical assets as IS/IT systems.

Business change cannot be managed as isolated and neatly bounded local implementations. Business processes are increasingly integrated and interlinked with an organisation's business information systems. Changes to either may affect the way staff work, possibly in more than

Chapter 3
Key principles

one business area. This means that only the senior operational managers are in a position to extract the value and benefits upon which the funding of the programme has been justified; and then only with the full commitment and involvement of managers and their staff.

It is recommended that overall authority and responsibility for the programme be assigned to a senior operational manager who will be accountable for the allocation of resources to the programme, managing the expenditure and above all ensuring that business benefits flow from the investment.

3.6 Key supporting roles

The authority and leadership of senior management must be supported by a team that manages the programme from day-to-day. The principles that guide the programme management organisation are expressed in three core sets of management responsibilities.

Management of the business change

At the heart of a programme is the vision of a new business operation and the benefits which that would bring. A *business change manager* is responsible for clarifying those benefits, managing their delivery through the programme's projects, and maximising the benefits realised in the future operations. By ensuring that each project contributes to the proposed benefits and that additional benefits come from the programme as a whole, this part of the programme management regime seeks to maximise the benefits identified in the programme's business case.

Management of the project portfolio

The second core responsibility is for efficient and effective management of multiple projects. By co-ordinating all project plans, managing the interfaces and dependencies between projects, efficiently sharing resources and speedily settling all issues of priority, the programme management team will help to minimise costs and the time taken to complete the programme.

The *programme manager* will be responsible for the overall progress of the programme of work within agreed funding and resource constraints. Certain development activities traditionally associated with individual projects may often be best carried out at the programme level – for example, project feasibility investigation.

Management of programme integrity

A programme will be initiated within the framework of the organisation's policies and architectures (for example for infrastructure such as IT or networking); but as individual projects are implemented, problems and conflicts may arise between effective progress and strict adherence to policies and architecture guidelines. Resolution of this type of potential conflict is the role of the *design authority*.

3.7 A framework to support change management

Senior managers who are made accountable for the outcome of a programme must be empowered to manage the programme successfully. However competent the personnel and however good the procedures at both project and programme levels, some things will go wrong, the unexpected will arise, and major changes may be called for. These major changes can only be effected if the managers are *informed* about the problems and if they are supported by a flexible management regime – that is, people and procedures.

Programme management requires a structure, style and culture, supported by working practices and procedures, that encourage the free flow of information across projects and to the top of the programme management organisation. There should be open sharing of issues and risk.

To help create the necessary flexible and well-informed regime, there should be active management of change and well-defined procedures for change control, conflict escalation and risk management.

Chapter 3
Key principles

There are also inherent tensions between the pressures to complete to time and budget, through project management disciplines, and the need to preserve the full scope of a programme and to adhere to policies and standards. Compromises will inevitably be required as the programme is implemented. These compromises, if they are left to individual Project Boards, may seriously prejudice attainment of the wider goals of the programme.

Because of the extended period of time for a programme and the initial lack of a detailed programme specification, it is necessary to give risk management a high profile within the framework of programme management. The risk management plan should contain a record of all risks, their possible impacts and what is to be done, and when, to reduce them to an acceptable level. Frequent reviews are needed and at the end of each major programme tranche risks should be reassessed.

4 Programme management activities

4.1 Four phases of activities In this approach to programme management, the activities required to manage a programme from its inception to successful conclusion are grouped into four phases, illustrated in Figure 3 below.

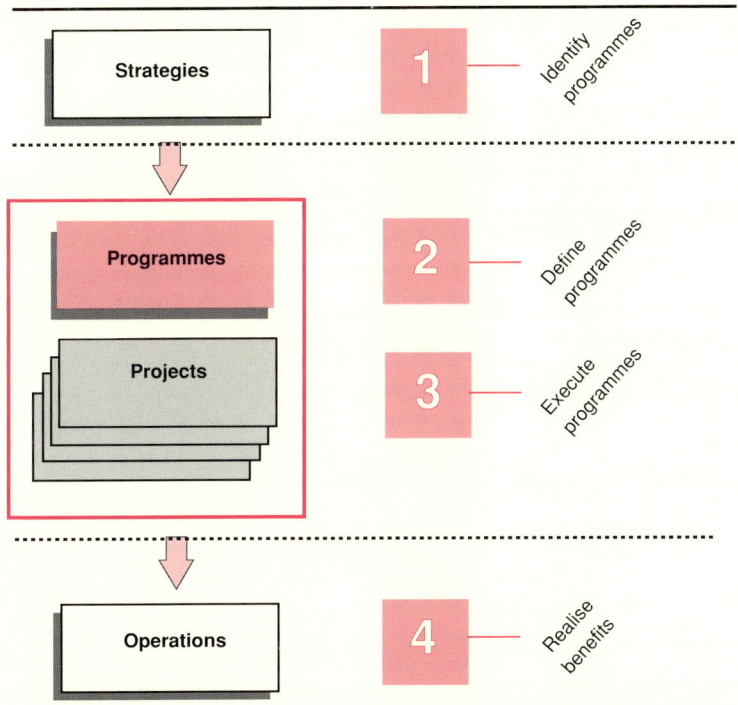

Figure 3 The phases of programme management

In the Programme Identification phase, the scope and boundaries of the programme are determined. The programme team then undertake detailed planning and initiation in the Programme Definition phase. The activities to co-ordinate and progress the multiple projects within the change programme are undertaken in the Programme Execution phase. In the Benefits Realisation phase, the activities focus on maximising the improvements from the changes put in place.

Typically, all four phases will be repeated within each tranche, although the first two phases may simply re-validate the programme's scope and definition, if the environment is relatively stable.

4.2 Phase 1 - Programme Identification

In programme identification, the senior management group considers the impact and benefit of all the changes proposed in their business strategy, or stemming from other initiatives, on the business operations and processes for which they are responsible; and decides whether to manage their implementation through one or more programmes.

This phase will normally form part of business planning and be led by members of a high level planning group, with input from custodians of policies and standards; operational support services providers, for example IT infrastructure management, personnel management, finance divisions; in-house resource providers, for example the IS development group and training divisions. Where these functions are being provided by third parties, some in-house capability should be retained to inform this planning activity. Such a capability is often described as an 'intelligent customer' function.

The main activities of the Programme Identification phase are to:

- identify relevant strategies and change initiatives; assess their impact on the business areas affected by them and define the benefits which are sought

- identify candidate groupings of projects and evaluate them for business benefits, economies of scale and compatibility with plans for support services such as IT infrastructure

- select as a programme the grouping of projects which achieves the best balance between strategic objectives and affordability, achievability and acceptable risk

- define and document each grouping as a programme and obtain authorisation for the business case

- appoint a Programme Director for each programme.

4.3 Phase 2 - Programme Definition

The Programme Director assumes responsibility for taking the implementation forward, including initiatives to improve awareness and communication. The Programme Director establishes the Programme Executive organisation (see Chapter 5) and produces a detailed Programme Definition Statement (from a programme feasibility study) before proceeding with execution of the programme. Although an overall programme typically has a timescale of three to five years or more, the prime focus for detailed planning should be on the next tranche of work and will normally aim to synchronise with financial planning cycles such as the Public Expenditure Survey (PES).

The main activities of this phase are to:

- establish an organisation structure and procedures to ensure the successful execution of the programme (in tranches, if appropriate)

- develop a Programme Definition Statement including the *blueprint*, a benefits management plan, risk management plan, and communications and awareness plan

- define Project Briefs for the first tranche of the programme

- develop further the business case for approval of funding at least to the end of the first tranche of programme execution

- establish the benefits management regime to ensure that the planned benefits will be measured and realised.

4.4 Phase 3 - Programme Execution

The execution of each tranche of the programme is concerned with reviewing and where necessary adjusting project plans and progress in the light of programme requirements. Programme execution focuses on changes in project interfaces; the smooth handover of project products to the business operation; and management of resources across projects.

The key players during this phase of the programme are the Programme Executive, who are likely to have their maximum workload during this period. They will be assisted by a Programme Support Office and will have frequent contact with the project management teams.

As outputs from projects are completed, the managers of the business operations need to become closely involved in the hand-over of these products into operational use, and in the accompanying transition activities to move into the improved modes of operation.

The main activities are to:

- manage the project portfolio
- manage the business transition activities
- monitor and maintain compliance with the programme design, corporate and programme architectures, policies and standards, and with infrastructure plans
- ensure programme-wide quality assurance and change control
- ensure that the effects of any changes in the programme plans, and also of any changed requirements arising externally to the programme, are being taken into account
- maintain the Programme Definition Statement
- monitor achievement towards the *blueprint* and against the business case
- take corrective actions in any of the above areas whenever necessary; for example define additional projects, close obsolete projects, replan.

4.5 Phase 4 - Benefits Realisation

By this phase, all projects in the current tranche will have been completed. A Programme Benefits Review should be undertaken at the end of each tranche of work formally to establish its achievement level. The Programme Benefits Review should be undertaken by a team reporting to the Programme Director, objectively analysing success and failure of the programme management process, as well as achievement of targets and performance levels.

The main activities of this phase are to:

- assess operational performance levels against objectives in the business *blueprint*
- ensure that all planned processes, and procedures of the *blueprint* are properly operational
- devise and implement compensating features for any shortfalls in the facilities delivered by the programme, if necessary by defining and implementing additional projects
- continue training and change activities as necessary
- seek additional areas of benefit from the exploitation of the delivered facilities
- fine tune the business operation
- ensure that lessons learned during the execution of the programme are fed back to strategy formulation and corrective actions taken before further tranches of the programme are executed.

After the execution of the final tranche, most of the resources assigned to the programme will have been redeployed. The operational environment will be stable (insofar as any business operation is ever stable) and in a position to exploit the new facilities.

5 Organising the programme

> The approach to organising a programme should ensure that all key responsibilities are clearly assigned. For a small programme these responsibilities may simply be expansions of existing roles, whilst in a large and complex programme, full-time roles, with additional support, will be justifiable. In either case make sure responsibilities are clearly defined and assigned.

The roles are concerned with two aspects of management, as shown in Figure 4 overleaf:

- authority and leadership: the Programme Director role
- day-to-day management: the Programme Executive roles

5.1 Programme Director role

The Programme Director has the overall responsibility for ensuring that the programme achieves the objectives that have been set and that the anticipated business benefits are realised. This responsibility is closely associated with the business case made for the programme funding.

The first objective of the Programme Director is to see that a new business operation of quality is created by the programme - one that business-area management is able to exploit to meet new levels of performance and new business needs. The Programme Director also ensures that the users and the organisation are managed carefully through the change process from the old operational business environment to the new, and that adjustments are made if this proves to be necessary to complete the changes.

The second objective of the Programme Director is to ensure that the aims of the programme and projects continue to be aligned with the evolving business needs. This involves determining project priorities, resolving conflicts regarding demands on resources, and agreeing additions, deletions or changes to the programme plan.

5.2 Programme Executive roles

The Programme Executive is a team, working to support the programme objectives and to minimise the risks, both to the programme's development schedule and to its eventual operational success. The composition of the Programme Executive is shown in Figure 4 opposite.

There will be tension between the responsibilities of the three key roles described in Chapter 3 (business change, programme management, design authority), focused respectively on:

- maximising the achievement of user and business needs as effectively as possible

- producing the programme deliverables as economically as possible, and on time

- ensuring the appropriate level of technical excellence, quality, and consistency.

It is important that these differing points of view are well understood and continually reassessed and reconciled. By explicitly recognising these tensions inherent in introducing change, the structure aims to manage them positively and creatively. Each role is described below.

5.3 Business Change Manager responsibilities

The Business Change Manager represents the Programme Director's interests in the final outcome of the programme, working with the senior people responsible for the business. The Business Change Manager's responsibilities will typically be:

- to identify, monitor and review the delivery of benefits

- to act as the guardian of the business case for the programme

- to take responsibility for 'management of change' activities so that transition is smooth

- to assume responsibility for management of risk.

Chapter 5
Organising the programme

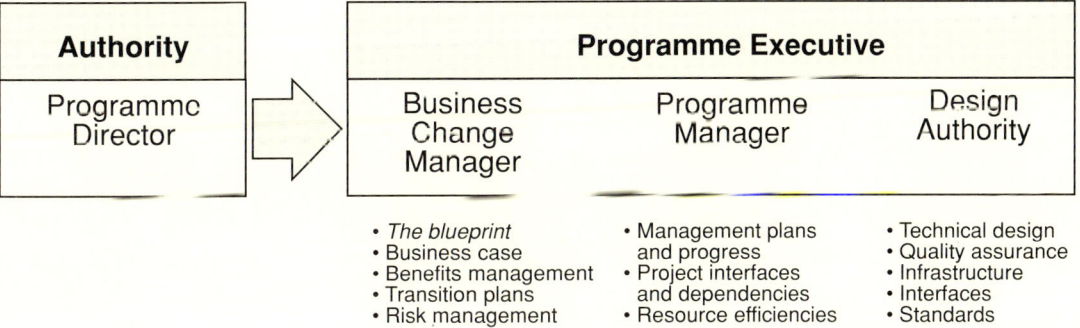

Figure 4 Programme management organisation

This role is responsible for the transition activities that will ensure that managers and staff in the business operation are taken along smoothly throughout the change programme and are fully prepared to exploit the new operational business environment, once it is in place.

The Business Change Manager is also the guardian of the business case for funding the programme of work. As implementation progresses the Business Change Manager is responsible for monitoring the business case, and confirming the continuing viability of the programme. It is suggested that the Business Change Manager also assumes overall responsibility for management of risk.

5.4 Programme Manager responsibilities

The Programme Manager carries out the day-to-day management of the programme. The Programme Manager's objectives should be to:

- ensure the delivery to time and against plan

- monitor overall progress and initiate corrective action as appropriate

- ensure efficiency in the allocation of common resources and skills within the projects portfolio

- manage dependencies and the interfaces between projects

- report progress of the programme to the Programme Director and senior management.

27

The Programme Manager's primary aim is to ensure the coherence of the programme and to develop and maintain the appropriate environment to support Project Managers within it.

5.5 Design Authority responsibilities

The primary concern of this role is to maintain the integrity of technical design throughout the portfolio of projects in the programme to ensure that:

- interfaces between projects are properly specified
- common project elements are recognised and no work is unnecessarily duplicated in different parts of the programme
- co-ordination and change control are applied to technical specifications and to the technical infrastructure
- quality assurance and testing of project deliverables are carried out satisfactorily
- business systems integration (involving, for example, end-to-end testing) is planned and managed.

The Design Authority should also act as custodian of infrastructure plans, technical designs, and management and technical policies and standards as they need to be applied within the programme.

5.6 Programme Support Office

A Programme Support Office is likely to be needed to collect, co-ordinate and analyse management information to support the Programme Executive. This management information will derive from both the programme management process and, in summarised form, from the projects. A Programme Support Office can serve both the programme and the individual projects, working with Project Support Offices where they are justified.

The Programme Support Office acts as a focus for all project reporting and control activities, and care must be taken with reporting mechanisms to ensure that bottlenecks do not result.

Chapter 5
Organising the programme

5.7 Roles at the boundaries of programme management

In the organisation structure illustrated in Figure 4, the Programme Director, who takes his or her authority from the Management Board or one of the Steering Committees responsible for specific areas of the business, delegates part of that authority to each of the Project Boards within the programme.

The structure is compatible with the operation of the CCTA project management method, PRINCE. The PRINCE Project Boards have authority within the scope of their Project Briefs and Project Managers have responsibility for managing their project's resources and activities.

6 Lessons from practical application

Some important lessons have emerged from practical application of this approach to programme management.

6.1 Identifying change points It is important to identify points during a programme, for example at the end of a tranche of work, when changes, even radical ones, can be made without sacrificing the investments already made. Ideally, these change points should be 'Islands of Stability' for all parties, as illustrated in Figure 2 in Chapter 3.

These change points must be convenient for both the business operation being changed and the people who are developing the changes.

6.2 Keeping the business operation running The business operation must be in a position to continue working efficiently, whilst still gaining the benefits from the changes delivered so far.

It must be possible to close down or redirect development activity without disastrous consequences for the business, for example unacceptable degradation of front-line customer services or support systems.

6.3 Scoping fundamental programmes Certain programmes may be deemed so fundamental that they should be ring-fenced and funded until their conclusion, to protect them from the impact of re-identification and major redefinition. The scope of such fundamental programmes should be carefully defined to ensure that only essential components are protected in this way.

6.4 Accommodating change Programme management arrangements must be prepared to accommodate even major changes as gracefully as possible.

Bibliography

CCTA has produced a range of publications which complement the guidance given in this volume. These publications are listed below.

Programme Management

'Managing Programmes of Large-Scale Change', a briefing pamphlet is available from the Library, CCTA, Riverwalk House, 157-161 Millbank, London SW1P 4RT.

A Programme and Project Management Library volume which describes the approach and how to apply it in more detail is available from HMSO through its bookshops and agents.

'A Guide to Programme Management'
ISBN: 0 11 330600 8

Information Systems Guides

The CCTA IS Guides are available from John Wiley and Sons Ltd., Baffins Lane, Chichester, PO19 1UD. Of particular interest are the following volumes:

IS Guide A2: *'Strategic Planning for Information Systems'*
ISBN: 0 471 92522 5

IS Guide A5: *'A Project Manager's Guide'*
ISBN: 0 471 92525 X

IS Guide B4: *'Appraising Investment in Information Systems'*
ISBN: 0 471 92529 2

IS Planning Subject Guides

These are available from the Library, CCTA, Riverwalk House, 157-161 Millbank, London SW1P 4RT. The following Guides will be of interest:

Managing and Controlling the IS Strategy
ISBN: 0 946683 40 9

Prioritisation
ISBN: 0 946683 44 1

Management of Change	A briefing pamphlet on this topic called *'Change for the Better?'* is available from the Library, CCTA, Riverwalk House, 157-161 Millbank, London SW1P 4RT.
Project Management	The CCTA-owned project management method PRINCE complements the approach described in this volume.
	The PRINCE reference manuals, published by NCC Blackwell (a five volume set), are available from NCC Ltd, Sales Administration (Publications), Oxford Road, Manchester, M1 7ED.
	ISBN: 1 85554 012 6
Quality	The CCTA Quality Management Library is available from HMSO through its bookshops and agents.
	ISBN: 0 11 330569 9
Risk Management	The CCTA Management of Risk Library is available from HMSO through its bookshops and agents.
	Introduction to the Management of Risk ISBN: 0 11 330603 2